香港國際詩歌之夜 *2011*
INTERNATIONAL POETRY NIGHTS IN HONG KONG

編輯 Editors

方梓勳 Gilbert C. F. Fong

陳嘉恩 Shelby K. Y. Chan

柯夏智 Lucas Klein

何潔賢 Amy Ho Kit Yin

北島 Bei Dao

田原

Tian Yuan

目錄 Contents

與鳥有關

飛來飛走
其實是鳥兒們自己的事情
但這一舉動總是牽動我的思緒
包括牠們有時聽起來像唱歌
又像慟哭的鳥鳴

陰霾的日子，牠們用翅膀馱來
遠方的陽光
暖亮我灰暗的內心
天若放晴
我陰冷的室內又因牠們的
啾鳴而充滿生氣

活着的鳥
見證着我的死亡
靜止在畫冊中的鳥
感受着我的鼻息和目光

即使在黑暗的夢中
鳥也猶如閃電的精靈
留下歌聲後隱去身影
讓我記不住牠們羽毛的顏色和眼睛

我常常面窗而坐
想像中的鳥
便帶領着一場暴雨而來

猛烈地抖動翅膀
像滂沱的雨滴
砸向大地

牠們常常飲水和洗足的河
變得乖戾
河灣瘋狂地長草
讓毒蛇的嘴潛伏其中
讓彎曲的河水流過樹冠
和枝丫間的鳥巢

而所有的這一切
都發生在一層透明的窗玻璃間
薄而脆弱的玻璃
是我與鳥和世界的距離

有一天，從樹頂上飛走的鳥
像一團火光
一閃即逝
牠留下的一聲長鳴
讓我平靜的心為之一驚

（2009年4月25日寫於日本）

Regarding Birds

Flying this way and that
Is just something birds do
But what they do tugs at my emotions
What with their chirps that can sound like singing
And sometimes like crying

On gloomy days their wings
bring a distant sunlight
Changing my inner grayness to a glow
And when the sky clears
My dim and drafty room fills
With the vitality of their warbling

Live birds
Are witnesses to my death
Motionless birds in a picture book
Sense my gaze and the breath from my nostrils

Even in dark dreams
Birds flash like fairies
leave behind song then disappear
Making me forget their eyes and color of their feathers

Often I often sit facing the window
Birds of the imagination
Bring a storm

Fiercely flapping their wings
Like a torrent of raindrops
Swooping to the earth

The river where they drink and wade
Shows its perverse temper
Grasses grow wildly at the river bend
Where serpents' fangs lurk
As the river winds beneath trees
And nests in the forks of branches

All of this takes place
In the space of a transparent windowpane
This thin layer of glass
Is the distance between me and the birds and the world

One day a bird flew from a treetop
Like a torch
Gone in a flash
It left behind a long cry
A note of surprise in my quiet mind

(Apr. 25, 2009—in Japan)

(Translated by Denis Mair)

盲流

至今，這個詞
還時常像一道極光
在我的記憶裏閃亮

那些年，我很年輕
像一匹健壯的馬
被時代看不見的鞭子
趕到了荒原

荒原上除了雜草叢生的野地外
也有幾座禿山
它們總是擋住我
遠眺的視線
讓我的鄉愁在荒原上
飄蕩。當然
禿山也阻擋着颶風
帶給我一種漂泊的安全感

那幢面朝南的
我住過一段時間的屋子
常常出現在我的夢中
依舊紅磚木窗
孤零零地忍受着風吹雨打
和狼嚎聲的恐嚇

就是在這座房屋前

我與盲流不期而遇
他來自山東
滿臉粗壯的鬍鬚讓我辨不出
他的年齡

有一天，我們混熟了
他送我從潛伏着怪物的湖裏
捕撈出的老頭兒魚
並小聲告訴我
他是一名逃犯

想起他眼神裏藏滿的恐懼
我就會看到
世界可怕的一面
我不清楚他犯有何罪

幾十年過去了
我突然想變成一匹馬
去荒原找他
哪怕找到的是
一堆白骨或一座墳墓

（2010年2月7日寫於日本）

Transient

Now and then this word
Flashes like a laser
in my memory

I was young in those years, like a sturdy horse
Driven by the era's invisible whip
into the wilderness

That prairie thick with wild grass
Was dotted with barren hills
They blocked
my distant gaze
And set my homesickness adrift
Across the waste spaces, yet the hills
Blocked out storms as well
Which gave me a floating sense of security

That little south-facing cottage
Where I lived for a time
Often appears in my dreams
The same slat-framed windows and red bricks
All alone enduring the weather
And fearsome howls of wolves

There in front of the cottage
A transient showed up one day

A man from Shandong
Behind his growth of whiskers
I could not tell his age

One day, after we got to know each other
He brought me a grand-daddy fish
He had caught in a haunted lake
And whispered to me
He was a fugitive

Thinking of the fear hidden in his eyes
I glimpsed the fearsome side
Of the world
I never knew his crime

Decades later
Suddenly I wish
I could be a horse
And search after him in the wilderness
Even if all I found was
A heap of white bones or a grave

(Feb. 7, 2010—in Japan)

(Translated by Denis Mair)

樓梯
——給畫家廣戶繪美[1]

陽光驅趕着樓梯上的黑暗
我感到時間的洪流
正順着樓梯瀉下
湮沒沉寂的空間

一只握着畫筆的手
如同擎着光芒
讓樓梯在黑暗中還原
把立體的現實變為平面的抽象

我為陽光在樓梯上的反光
感動。人生多麼像
那飄動在反光裏的雲朵啊
隨着太陽的移動，變幻消失
然後，又隨太陽的升起而重現

樓梯是一種秩序和規律
把奧秘深藏在它的哲學裏
樓梯是一種沉默
它默默地承受着黑暗和孤獨的壓迫

樓梯有很多種結構和質地
陡和緩，寬和窄，木頭和水泥等等
但它們屬行的職責只有一種
上：縮短你與太陽的距離

下：讓你走進地平線或遼闊的大地

樓梯是一道暗器
停電的夜晚，我們不得不小心翼翼地
用腳步試探着它攀緣
樓梯也是一把椅子，有時
供我們坐着歇息或生悶氣

我們常常忽視樓梯的存在
其實，人人心中都有一個樓梯
它時時考驗着我們：
是否上得去還能下得來

（2010年1月16日寫於日本）

譯者註：

1. 廣戶繪美（Hiroto Emi，1981-）日本當代超寫實主義畫家。現居北海道。

Stairway
— for Hiroto Emi, painter

Sunlight chases away the darkness of a stairway
I sense the floodtide of time
Pouring down the staircase
To engulf the silent spaces

A hand holds a paintbrush
As if wielding a beam of light
Out of darkness restoring a stairway
Abstracting solid reality into two dimensions

I am moved by reflection of sunlight
In the stairway. Our life is much like
This cloud of sunlit motes
Shifting along with a beam, a vanishing figment
Then reappearing with the rising sun

A stairway is order and pattern
Concealing deep secrets in its philosophy
A stairway is a kind of silence
Bearing the weight of darkness and solitude

A stairway is replete with structure and texture
Such as gradient, width, whether wood or cement
But it carries out only one duty
Up: to shorten your distance from the sun

Downward: you walk into the horizon or the vast
    landscape

A stairway is a concealed weapon
On nights the power's out, we have to proceed carefully
feeling our way up the stairs with our feet
A stairway can also be a chair—sometimes
offering us a seat to rest on, or to brood on

We often overlook the existence of stairs
In fact, in each person's heart is a stairway
testing us always:
if we go up will we be able to come down?

(Jan. 16, 2010—in Japan)

(Translated by Denis Mair)

小鎮

循着敘述壟斷的記憶
南下，在臨水的小鎮上
一聲邂逅的狗叫
喚起我的羈愁

毀於兵燹的木樓被文字還原
清澈的水裏
魚鱗帶着那時的星光
在水底閃亮

隔着那麼長的歲月
河流是一條疲憊的繃帶
它包紮着受傷的村落和山崗
滄桑的碼頭
翹望一片粼粼之水
彷彿在等待消瘦的水手
伴隨着一陣陣咳嗽
划着烏篷船
逆流而歸

挺拔的老樹上
嘰嘰喳喳的麻雀
數着青石路上的跫音
殘破的古廟裏
圓寂的和尚夢見天堂

隱隱約約傳來的船歌
回蕩在下游
載動船的水
卻流不走
那夾雜在天籟裏的咳嗽

無遮無攔的天
是一面鏡子
反照出記憶的黑斑
一個時代的倒影
在水中晃動
變得模糊不清

旅次小鎮
在陌生感被黑暗沖淡的夜晚
我在夢中咳血
然後夢見
老水手那明明滅滅的煙袋鍋
照亮我的臉

（2009年4月26日寫於日本）

Small Town

Heading south, along memories monopolized
By narrative, in a little waterfront town
Encountering a barking dog
Stirs my suppressed sorrows

A pillaged farmhouse restored by writing
Deep in a crystalline pond
The era's starlight on fish scales
Gleaming under water...

Across such a gulf of years
The river is a weary bandage
Enwrapping the wounded village and hills
A weathered dock looks out on rippling reflections
As if waiting for a haggard boatman
With an intermittent cough
To row his dark-sailed boat
Back upstream

In an upright old tree
A few chirping sparrows
Counting footfalls on flagstones
In a dilapidated temple
The deceased monk dreams of nirvana

The boatman's faint song reverberates downstream
But the water bearing the boat
Cannot carry away the coughing
Tangled in the music of nature

Heaven laid bare
Is a mirror
Reflecting blemishes of memory
An era's inverted reflections
Wavering in the water, growing indistinct

At a little town along the way
One night when unfamiliarity is diluted by darkness
I cough up blood in a dream
And then dream of
the old boatman
The intermittent glow of his pipe
lighting up my face

(Apr. 26, 2009—in Japan)

(Translated by Denis Mair)

深夜

樹木們假寐着生長
星星的絮語依舊璀璨
像一椿透明的往事

夢遊症患者在平房的醫院牆外
狂奔。像一匹剽悍的野驢
他的高喊使醫生病倒
如同患了絕症

漁火明滅在夢的盡頭
船頭上，漁民解開魚鷹脖子上的繩
將魚鷹的腳拴綁在船尾
魚鷹的翅膀抖落的水珠
淋濕星星

船走破了鞋，生鏽的錨
思念着故鄉的碼頭
雲在雲裏酣睡
夢見軟綿綿的枕頭開花
開出時間的顏色

深夜是屬於大海的
它無底的沉默似一種寬容
承受着鼓帆的飄動
河流向河，山蜿蜒着山

水和石頭的胳膊
挽緊着大地

夜空錄下了處女的夢話
和牙齒的磨擦聲
稻草人被繃得緊緊的腿
跳着獨步舞
在大地的裂縫裏深入淺出
汗水淹沒的欲望裏
女人被壓迫的聲音
使夜更深

其實，黑暗的深處是碧藍的
像豐秋沉甸甸的一句祝福
像子宮裏打盹的胎兒的心

(2001年5月13日寫於日本)

Late at Night

The trees doze while growing
Sweet nothings of stars still sparkle
Like the transparent past

A sleepwalker sprints outside the one-store
Hospital, like a headstrong feral donkey
His yawp makes the doctor keel over
Like he has caught something terminal

A fishing lantern flickers at dream's edge
On the boat, the fisherman unties the cormorant's halter
He fastens it by a long line to the stern
Water droplets shaken by the cormorant's wings
Wet the stars

The worn-out shoes of the boat, its rusty anchor
Yearn for the dock of its native land
Clouds fast asleep within clouds
Dream of blossoms from downy pillows
Blooming with colors of the season

The night belongs to the ocean
Its bottomless silence like a forgiveness
That accepts the vagaries of sail-bellying winds
The river flows to the river
Mountains meander to mountains

Arms of stone and water
Lay across the earth

The night sky records a virgin's sleep talk
And gritting teeth
The scarecrow's tight-stretched legs
dance a solo
And sum up profundities from the earth's cracks
In sweat-drowned desire
Women's oppressed voices
Make the night later and deeper

In fact, the depths of darkness are royal blue
Like a fruitful blessing in ripe autumn
Like the heart of a fetus sleeping in the womb

(May 13, 2001—in Japan)

(Translated by Denis Mair)

鋼琴

在我看來
鋼琴很像一匹怪獸的骨架
高貴地佔據着城市的一角

其實，它乃平民出身
最初與城市的拱頂、玻璃窗
燕尾服及拖地裙無關
它的骨骼和神經、呼吸和眼神
緊繫着鄉村

鋼琴的轟鳴是鄉村一棵大樹上的聲音
也與蟲子在田野裏的歌唱
非常接近

不只是荷蘭、莫斯科和巴黎才是它的故鄉
荒涼的大地和烏雲密布的天空
也同樣隱藏着它的夢想
當風撞死在船帆上
錨在水中生鏽
當手指按出的聲音
被稱做音樂
……

鋼琴無奈地調節着城市人的心情
無奈地擺脫着購置者的擺弄
一種被虛榮擺設的處境

使它清潤高貴的嗓音漸漸變啞
最終像被送進火葬場的城市人
被焚燒成灰燼

弦是頭髮
鍵是牙齒
音槽是嘴唇

鋼琴總使我緬想起遠離城市的樹木
被伐倒後豁然闊朗的天空
和樹木被刨去根後
遺留在大地上的深坑

在我看來
鋼琴在城市僅僅是裝飾的圖圖
它很想變成一匹怪獸
長出翅膀，飛逃

（2000年7月12日寫於日本）

Piano

The way I see it
The piano is like the skeleton of a strange beast
That aristocratically occupies a corner of the city

Actually, it was a commoner by birth
It used to have nothing to do with domes or window glass
Or tuxedoes and floor-length gowns
Its bone structure and nerves, its breath and gaze
were bound tightly to the country village

A piano's roar is the sounds of a country tree
And is quite close
To songs of the meadow

It is not just native to Holland or Moscow or Paris
Desolate plains and dark clouds covering the sky
hide its dreams too
When the wind expires against a sail
an anchor rusts underwater
When flexing fingers make a sound
called music
......

The piano can't help but fine tunes city-dwellers' moods
Can't help but break away from purchasers manipulations
Caught in a predicament of vain display

Its plangent notes hoarsen
Like a city dweller taken to the crematorium
burned to ash

The strings are hair
Its keys teeth
the sound board is a mouth

The piano makes me think of a trees far from the city
the wide open sky after it is felled
and the deep hole left
After it's uprooted

As I see it
A piano in the city is nothing but an ornamented jail
The piano wants to become a strange beast
grow wings and fly away

(July 12, 2000—in Japan)

(Translated by Denis Mair)

如歌的行板

你臉上的早晨在太陽升起時
退去。目光裏的曙色泛着淺黃
門前的樹木在一夜間高過了房屋
千里之外的河流在汛期將帆影和船歌淹沒

清晨，看不見的年輪像音盤
在樹心裏鳴響。鷙鷹叼着人骨
去太陽火化。樹杈間的鴉巢
着火。室內的海螺標本裏
濺出了濤聲

漲潮了
我的手指在漲潮後沾滿你生命的芳香
我的夜晚落在你的大山之間
鳥聲壓彎山脊和壓低你的聲音
鳥聲讓蓬勃兩個季節的草原枯死

黑暗在我罪惡的手指上燃燒
熊熊烈焰裏，一萬次過去是一萬束花朵
在你的右眼裏凋謝枯萎

生活本來就是一棵瘋長的樹木
它頂破天空。水自天而降
溺死樹木。我在一場洪水裏
被你隨便摘下的一片樹葉救起

我乘着一片樹葉，盼望着洪水
退去的日子

岸就這樣的誕生了
它柔嫩得像嬰兒的膚肌
草的根扎進岸邊泥土下的沙子裏
結出大海和大河的秘密

你和我都是岸邊含苞待放的籽粒
被風吹開，被鳥銜走
在離水很遠的陸地和大山深處長大
然後被漂浮的島嶼運載到一起

是誰在黑暗裏遮掩着面孔
讓病菌在指甲裏長大，然後
像跳蚤和虱子在我們的皮膚和衣縫上產卵
讓我的皮膚鬆弛，讓你的乳房乾癟

我曾在你的黎明裏懷念夜晚
像露珠和薄霧被陽光拾起投扔給黃昏
你曾在夜晚裏渴望抵達我的黎明
像星星和漁火企圖將黑暗燃破

是誰用食指輕壓住我的嘴唇
是誰在用纖弱的手指將你一層一層剝開

像剝開玉米棒子
你赤裸裸的皓齒泛着成熟的光芒
我被你瘋狂而又抒情地嚼動

我的房屋因此燃燒成褐色的雲
我跑在風的前頭躲在你飄動的裙下
變小着自己。我多想是一滴液體的
生命，游動在你溫暖的子宮

夢是黑色的
青春是黑色的
未來和歷史是黑色的
死亡是黑色的

（1999年2月16日）

Andante Cantabile

The morning that appears in your face vanishes
with the rising of the sun. Dawn that shone in your eyes
    turns yellow.
Overnight the tree by the gate grows higher than the house.
A thousand miles away a river deepens and inundates
    sails and ships' songs.

By morning unseen growth rings resound in the core of a tree
like phonograph records. An eagle bearing a human bone
    in its beak
ascends towards the sun for cremation. In a tree's crotch
    a crow's nest
catches fire. Loud wave sounds splash out
from a conch specimen in the room.

It's high tide.
My fingers grow moist with the fragrance of your life
and my night sinks between your hills.
Birds' voices warp the mountain's spine, make you whisper,
and wither the grasslands that have thrived for two
    seasons.

Darkness burns on my guilty fingertips.
In the rising flames, ten thousand pasts become a
    thousand bouquets,
which droop and die in your right eye.

Daily living is essentially a succulent shoot
which can shoot up through the sky. Water pours from the
     heavens
and drowns the trees. Beset by the flood
I am saved by a single tree leaf that you have casually
     plucked.
Riding on that leaf
I wait for the water to recede.

And so a river bank was born,
as soft as a baby's skin.
Grass sinks roots into the sand beneath the mud of the bank,
thus rendering fruitful the sea's and the river's secrets.

Both you and I are buds on the bank about to open.
Blown away by the wind and picked up by birds
we grow on land far away from water and deep in the
     mountains,
and are carried away to floating islands to cohabit again.

Who on earth is that
covering his face in darkness,
breeding germs under his nails,
laying eggs like fleas and lice between our skin and
     clothing,
making my skin sag and withering your breasts?

At your dawn I fondly recollect the night.
Like dew drops and filmy mist which are picked up by
sunlight and cast into twilight,
so you who are night eagerly await my arrival at daybreak,
just as stars and fishing lights endeavor to obliterate the
darkness.

Who softly pressed my lips with a forefinger?
Who peeled you layer by layer with his thin fingers
like an onion?
Your bared white teeth emit mature light
and I am masticated by your lyricism, that approaches
madness,

so that my room burns and turns into a brown cloud.
Running before the wind, hiding within your billowing skirt,
I make myself ever smaller. How I wish I could turn into a
drop of liquid life
and keep swimming in your warm womb!

Dreams are black.
Youth is black.
The future and history are black.
Death also is black.

(Feb.16,1999)

(Translated by William I. Elliott and Kazuo Kawamura)

墳墓

幾只啾鳴的鳥
驚破周圍的寂靜
棲落在墳頂

一陣陣涼風
一把把無形的木梳
梳彎墳上的枯草

死去的人被運來葬下
悲傷和回憶
從此在這裏落戶扎根

活着的人走來
在墓碑前輕輕合掌
留下腳印離去

沙漠是駱駝的墳墓
大海是水手的墳墓
地球是文明的墳墓

墳墓是死亡的另一種形狀
像美麗的乳房
隆起在大地的胸膛

靜止的墳墓也在成長
但它從不挪動自己的位置
即使被洪水漫過被風沙湮埋

墳墓
是長在地平線上的耳朵
聆聽和分辨着它熟悉的跫音

（2007年5月3日從沖繩旅行歸來）

A Grave

A few chirping birds
break the surrounding tranquility
and alight on the grave.

A cool wind,
like an invisible wooden comb,
combs the dead grass on the grave.

The dead are carried off and buried
and from that moment sadness and memory
take root there.

The living come,
clasp their hands before the monument
and depart, leaving their footprints.

The desert is the camel's grave.
The sea is the sailors' grave.
But earth is the grave of civilization.

The grave is another shape of death.
It rises like a beautiful breast
above earth's breast.

Standing there, the grave also grows up,
even in a fierce flood,

even though subjected to storms and buried under sand.

The grave is
ears raised by the horizon.
It distinguishes whose footsteps they are.

(May 3, 2007—returned from Okinawa)

(Translated by William I. Elliott and Kazuo Kawamura)

詩人、文學博士。1965年生於河南漯河，90年代初赴日留學，現在日本國立東北大學任教。先後出版過《田原詩選》（人民文學出版社2007年）等五本詩集。在台灣、中國國內和美國獲得過華文詩歌文學獎，2001年用日語創作的三首現代詩獲日本第一屆「留學生文學獎」。在日本出版有日語詩集《岸的誕生》（思潮社2004年）和《石頭的記憶》（思潮社2009年），後者獲日本2010年度第60屆「H氏詩歌大獎」。主編有日文版《谷川俊太郎詩選集》（集英社文庫版三卷2005年）。在國內、新加坡、香港翻譯出版有《谷川俊太郎詩選》(河北教育出版社2004年)、《異邦人——辻井喬詩選》(人民文學出版社2005年)、《春的臨終——谷川俊太郎詩選》(香港牛津大學出版社2010年)。發表有中、短篇小說和大量的日語論文。編選有兩冊日文版《中國新生代詩人詩選》（竹內新譯，詩學社2004年）等。出版有文論集《谷川俊太郎論》(岩波書店2010年)等。

Born in 1965 in Henan Province, China, Tian Yuan first came to Japan as a government-financed student early in the 1990's. In 2003, he received a Doctorate in Literature for his study of the poetry of Shuntarō Tanikawa. He now teaches in Tōhoku University in Japan, and is chiefly engaged in the translation of contemporary Japanese poetry. His books of translation into Chinese so far include *Selected Poems of Shuntarō Tanikawa* (2 volumes) and *An Alien: Selected Poems of Takashi Tsujii*. He has also translated some poems of Ryuichi Tamura and Katsuei Kitazono. He has published six volumes of his own poetry in Chinese and English. He has been awarded literary prizes for poetry in China, America and Taiwan, and in 2001, he was awarded the first Japanese Literary Award for Foreign Students. His book of poetry in Japanese *And So the Shore Was Born* (*Sōshite Kishi ga Tanjōshita*) was published in 2004. He is the editor of the 3 volumes of *The Selected Poems of Shuntarō Tanikawa* (Shueisha, 2005). The second poetry anthology of *The Memory of Stone* was awarded the 60th session of H-shi Prize (2010). He also edited the Japanese version of *The Anthology of Chinese New Generation Poets* translated by Shin Takeuchi. Last year, *Selected Poems of Tian Yuan* (Renmin Wenxue, 2007) was published in Chinese.

出版 Publisher
香港中文大學出版社 The Chinese University Press

封面及平面設計 Cover and Graphic Designer
朱德華 Almond Chu

製稿及分色 Art Work and Colour Separation
明星鐳射分色有限公司 Star Laser Graphic Co. Ltd.

印刷 Printer
宏亞印務有限公司 Asia One Printing Ltd.

出版日期 Date of Publication
二零一一年十月 October 2011

國際書號 ISBN
978-962-996-526-6

香港國際詩歌之夜2011主辦單位
International Poetry Nights in Hong Kong 2011 Organizers

香港中文大學東亞研究中心
Centre for East Asian Studies, The Chinese University of Hong Kong

香港城市大學人文社會科學院
College of Liberal Arts and Social Sciences, City University of Hong Kong

香港科技大學人文社會科學學院
School of Humanities and Social Science,
The Hong Kong University of Science and Technology

香港國際詩歌之夜2011協辦單位
International Poetry Nights in Hong Kong 2011 Co-organizer
木刻文化出版有限公司 MUKE Publishing Limited